C000276854

ISBN 978-1-5282-0840-6
PIBN 10912639

FB &c Ltd, Dalton House, 60 Windsor Avenue, London, SW19 2RR.
Company number 08720141. Registered in England and Wales.

For support please visit www.forgottenbooks.com

SELECT LIST

GLADIOLI, DAHLIAS, ROSES, HARDY PLANTS and SHRUBS

SPRING 1920

Grown and for sale by

N. A. HALLAUER

ONTARIO, N. Y.

TELEPHONE 17-F-23

Announcement

In issuing this new catalogue for the spring of 1920, I take great pleasure in thanking my many friends for their generous patronage in the past and I hope to merit a continuance of their patronage.

I am always glad to welcome visitors to my gardens who are interested in hardy plants and flowers. My gardens are located on the improved Ridge Road 17 miles from Rochester. Rochester and Sodus Bay car—Stop 60 is directly in front of the premises. It is only about five minutes' walk from Fruitland Station on the R. W. & O. R. R.

TO MY PATRONS—I shall be glad at any time to make suggestions as to the selection of varieties of plants or shrubs for any given purpose or to assist in making up collections of either standard varieties of plants or of novelties. I shall undertake to secure at reasonable prices any plant or shrub for my patrons, which I may not have in my large collection. Information relating to the culture of special plants will be frankly and freely given at any time.

GUARANTEE—If I hope to retain trade, I can send only such stock as is true to name, first-class quality and in good condition when it leaves my place. Since I have no control over stock after it leaves my place, I cannot assume responsibility for failures due to improper planting or neglect after the plants have left my hands. I guarantee safe arrival of all stock sent by express. I also guarantee all stock true to name, and in a healthy growing condition when it leaves my hands. Any stock which proves otherwise will be gladly replaced or the price therefor refunded. I never substitute inferior varieties for those ordered, but should a variety ordered be sold out, I will fill the order with a similar or better variety, correctly labeled, unless instructions to the contrary are given in the order.

The prices quoted in this list are as low as is consistent with the quality of stock we send out. In some cases, our prices will be found lower than prices quoted by others, but in no case will we send out any stock except of the highest quality.

When ordering, please write your **name, postoffice, county and state** plainly and give your nearest express office address, if it is different from your postoffice address.

It is **very important to order early.** Our stock of some of the choicest varieties is limited and it is often impossible to secure them late in the season.

Cut Flowers—During the blooming season we can generally supply fancy cut flowers of Iris, Peonies, Gladioli, Dahlias and other hardy plants.

Kindly send me the names of your flower loving friends. I shall be glad to send them copies of my catalogue and will repay you by including extras with your order.

Make all remittances payable to

N. A. HALLAUER, Ontario, N. Y.

Gardens and American Express Office, Fruitland, N. Y.

Gladioli

Gladioli are of very easy culture. The bulbs may be planted as early as the ground can be worked and for a succession of bloom every two weeks up to July. The ground should be dug deeply and the bulbs planted 4 to 6 inches deep. They may be planted in rows 1 foot apart and 5 to 6 inches apart in the rows. A sandy loam soil away from the shade of trees or buildings, suits them best, although they will thrive in any good garden soil.

	Ea.	Doz.	100
AMERICA—Large, clear lavender pink. The best pink	$ .05	$ .50	$ 3.50
ATTRACTION—Large, rich, dark crimson; clear white throat	.05	.50	
AUGUSTA—Pure white, blue anthers	.05	.50	3.50
AZALEA (Kundred)—White ground color, striking throat markings. Ruffled	.25	2.50	
BARON HULOT—Rich, deep indigo blue. The best blue	.10	1.00	
BERTREX—White with lilac lines in throat. Size and form of America. Tall straight spike. New	.20	2.00	
BLANCHE—White, faint markings, very large	.15	1.50	
BLUE JAY—Pale blue, with white blotch; large	.30	3.00	
BRENCHLEYENSIS—Vermillion scarlet. An old but popular variety	.05	.50	3.00
CANARY BIRD—Pure Canary yellow. One of the best	.10	1.00	8.00
CHICAGO WHITE—White, faint throat markings, early	.05	.50	4.00
CRACKER JACK—Large, dark red, mottled throat	.05	.50	2.50
DAWN (Tracy's)—Long spike of a beautiful coral pink	.10	1.00	
EMPRESS OF INDIA—Rich, deep purplish crimson. Very attractive	.10	1.00	5.00
EUROPA—The finest pure white. Massive spikes of extra large flowers	.25	2.50	12.00
EVELYN KIRTLAND—New. The flowers of strong substance, are a beautiful shade of rosy pink, darker at the edges, fading to shell pink at the center, with brilliant scarlet blotches on lower petals. Wide open flowers, slightly fluted and many open at a time. Very tall, straight spikes. One of the finest	.30	3.00	
FAUST—Deep velvety crimson. Large flowers on a very tall spike	.10	1.00	
GLORY (Kundred)—Creamy white, crimson stripe in lower petals. Large and fine Ruffled	.10	1.00	6.00
GOLDEN KING—Bright golden yellow, with large crimson blotch on lower petal	.10	1.50	10.00
GOLDEN WEST—Clear orange scarlet; lower petals shaded golden yellow. Fine for exhibition	.15	1.50	
GRETCHEN ZANG—New. The blossoms are large and sparkling, and the most beautiful soft melting shade of pink, blending into scarlet on the lower petals. The color everyone wants. Spike tall and graceful	.25	2.50	

	Ea.	Doz.	100
HALLEY—Delicate salmon pink, creamy blotch on lower petals with red stripe..	.05	.50	4.00
HERADA—New. Another good one. Blooms of immense size on tall straight spikes. Massive in every way. The large blooms are pure mauve, glistening and clear, with deeper markings in the throat. A very striking and attractive color......	.20	2.00	
IDA VAN (Kunderd)—Brilliant orange red, large and showy	.10	1.00	
INDEPENDENCE—Light scarlet with richly marked throat. One of the best for cutting................................	.05	.50	2.50
IVORY Kunderd)—Ivory white with light markings. Ruffled	.20	2.00	
LIEBESFEUER—Brilliant scarlet. One of the finest and richest colored.............	.20	2.00	
LILY LEHMAN—Pure white. Lily form..	.10	1.00	
LOVLINESS—Creamy white, robust strong grower; dark green foliage...........	.15	1.50	9.00
MARY FENNELL—Light lavender, lower petals penciled yellow	.25	2.50	
MASTER WIETZE—Beautiful dark violet; a new variety	.20	2.00	15.00
MAY—White; finely flaked with bright rosy crimson	.05	.60	3.50
MEPHISTOPHLES—Dark red, stained black and yellow	.15	1.50	
MRS. DR. NORTON—White edged, soft pink yellowish blotch	1.00		
MRS. FRANCES KING—Flame pink, a very tall spike, flowers very large	.05	.50	3.50
MRS. FRANK PENDLETON, JR. (Kunderd). Very large wide open flowers, bright salmon pink with blood red blotch on lower petals. Very attractive	.10	1.00	5.50
MYRTLE (Kunderd)—Delicate rose pink with creamy throat. Very pretty.......	.20	2.00	
NIAGARA—Soft creamy yellow, splashed with carmine. A seedling of America, which it resembles, but is larger........	.10	1.00	6.00
PANAMA—Another seedling of America but is larger, taller and of a deeper color. A prize winner	.10	.75	5.00
PEACE—Very large white with faint markings on lower petals	.10	.75	5.00
PINK PERFECTION—La France Pink. Large open flowers. One of the best....	.15	1.50	
PRIMULINUS HYBRIDS—Beautiful shades of yellow and orange. Very graceful....	.05	.50	
PRIDE OF HILLEGON—Bright scarlet; very large	.50	5.00	
PRINCE OF WALES—Pale salmon; self color; large and early	.25	2.50	
PRINCEPS—Amaryllis-like flowers, rich scarlet with conspicuous white blotches on lower petals. Very large..........	.05	.50	4.50
RED EMPEROR—Clear, blood red. A very large flower on a long spike...........	.30	3.00	
SCHWABEN—Delicate pale yellow, dark blotch. Very large flower and spike..	.10	1.00	7.00
SCRIBE—White, freely flaked carmine. Very large flower on a long spike............	.10	1.00	
SUMMER BEAUTY (Kunderd)—Clear pink. Very tall spike. Very choice	.25	2.50	
WAR—Deep blood red, shaded darker. Tall spike. Very attractive	.15	1.50	

WHITE GIANT—Pure white, very large flower on long spike, early..............	.50	5.00	
WILLY WIGMAN—White, with dark crimson blotch	.10	1.00	
ALL COLORS MIXED—A choice mixture of Silver Trophy, to which have been added some choice named varieties. All good..		.40	2.50
MIXED SEEDLINGS—Selected seedlings of my own raising. Not a poor variety among them. Impossible to obtain a better collection of choice varieties for the money		1.00	7.00

Gladiolus bulbs at the each and dozen prices are sent postpaid; at the 100 price they are sent by express. 6 at the dozen rate and 25 at 100 rate.

Dahlias

CULTURE—The Dahlia will grow in any good garden soil. The soil should be worked deep and well prepared. Large quantities of manure should be avoided, as it tends to produce a heavy growth of foliage at the expense of bloom. An application of bone meal or good commercial fertilizer will generally be found sufficient. The roots should be planted 2½ feet apart in rows 3 feet apart. They should be laid down flat and covered with four or five inches of soil. They may be planted as soon as frost is over, but in our climate we have found June the best month to plant them out. In case the plants become stunted by hot, dry weather cut them back so that they will produce new wood for the cool months of autumn.

After the plants have been frozen in the fall, dig carefully and store the roots in a dry, cool cellar for winter. In the spring, the roots should be divided, preferably to one eye, before planting.

We list only those varieties which we can recommend and which have been selected from our large collection.

CLASSIFICATION OF DAHLIAS

CACTUS DAHLIAS—These are of recent introduction and are becoming very popular. In form they somewhat resemble the Chrysanthemum, the petals are long, narrow, incurved and sometimes twisted, giving them a very graceful appearance.

DECORATIVE DAHLIAS are the largest flowering of any type. They have long, broad, flat petals.

SHOW DAHLIAS are the old-fashioned large, round compact and quillled flowered type.

FANCY DAHLIAS are show Dahlias, having the flowers tipped or edged lighter than the ground color.

PEONY FLOWERED DAHLIAS are the newest type, and somewhat resemble the peony in form. The flowers are generally semi-double, exposing golden yellow disc in the center. They are very beautiful and free flowering.

POMPON DAHLIAS are identical in form with show dahlias but are small.

SINGLE DAHLIAS have a single row of petals surrounding a golden yellow center. They are very graceful and free flowering.

COLLARETTE DAHLIAS are single Dahlias having a row of petals inside of the outside row.

Cactus Dahlias

	Each
AMBASSADOR—Pure white, beautiful form	.20
AURORA—Soft pink, tinted white overlaid gold, early and free	.25
BIANCA—Very large, rose lilac with white shadings.....	1.00
CLARA G. STREDWICK—Clear salmon shaded yellow....	.20

Each

COUNTESS OF LONSDALE—Deep salmon pink. Very free. Good cutting variety .... .20

COUNTESS OF MALMESBURY—Delicate peach pink, long, narrow petals .... .25

CREPUSELE—Very full, pale orange yellow, shaded fawn. Very good .... .25

CRYSTAL—Very large, long, narrow, incurved petals. Clear, soft pink. Good exhibition variety .... .50

EARL OF PEMBROKE—Rich plum color. Large and free .10

FLAG OF TRUCE—Large, pure white.... .20

FLORA—One of the best pure white, very free.... .20

FLORADORA—Dark red, fine form. Very free. One of the best .... .20

GEN. BULLER—Deep red, tipped white. Very free.... .15

GEORGE WALTERS—Very large, hybrid cactus, salmon pink, shading to yellow a tthe base of the petals, one of the largest 1.50

GOLDEN GATE—Bright, golden yellow; early and free flowering; very large, often measuring 9 inches.... .25

GOLDEN GEM—Golden yellow. Very attractive. One of the best .... .30

GOLDEN EAGLE—Yellow, slightly tinged fawn. Very large .30

HARBOR LIGHT—Bright orange red, overlaid flame color .15

H. SHOESMITH—Brilliant, vermillion scarlet .... .20

ICEBERG—Ivory, white large, good form .... .20

INDOMNITABLE—Long, narrow, incurved petals. Rosy mauve, tipped lighter .... .50

JEANETTE—Fine buttercup yellow. One of the best.... .50

J. H. JACKSON—Rich velvety maroon. Very large. One of the best dark ones .... .15

KALIF—Rich crimson, very large, long stems; very free. One of the best .... .60

KRIEMHILDE—Rosy pink, with white center. Very pretty .15

MASTER CARL—Bright orange salmon. Large and handsome .... .30

MARGUERITE BOUCHON—One of the finest pink exhibition Dahlias. Brilliant rose-pink with a delicate white center. Very large on long stems.... .50

MME. HENRI CAYEUX—Rich pink, tipped white. Very large, narrow, incurved florets .... .30

MRS. DE LUCA—Yellow, shaded orange.... .15

MRS. J. H. JONES—Bright scarlet tipped white.... .20

MRS. J. EMBERSON—Pale lemon speckled rose pink. Very attractive .... .25

MAD. H. MARTINET—Yellow, shaded old gold and pink .30

MRS. WARNAAR—Very large, creamy white, shaded pink. A new variety of great merit.... 1.00

REINE CAYEUX—Medium sized flowers, rich geranium red. Always good .... .25

STANDARD BEARER—Bright scarlet. One of the best.. .15

RHEINKONIG—Pure white. Very large and free.... .35

WINSOME—Large, creamy white.... .25

WODAN—Beautiful salmon rose, shading to old gold at the center. Very large, semi-incurved form.... .35

WOLFGANG VON GOETHE—Rich apricot, shaded carmine. Very large .... .35

YVONNE CAYEUX—Pure white. Large, perfect form. Very fine .... .35

Decorative Dahlias

ALICE ROOSEVELT—Large white, overlaid lilac, good cut flower variety .... $ .35

AMERICAN BEAUTY—Wine crimson, immense size and very free. The best of its color.... .20

Very large, long stems and free ... .50

BREEZELAWN—Very large, of perfect form, fiery vermillion ... 1.50

CLIFFORD W. BRUTON—Bright yellow. Very large ... .15

CATHERINE DUER—Bright crimson scarlet, free ... .10

CREATION—Large, full flowers on long stems, cherry red suffused bronze ... 1.00

DELICE—Clear pink, long stems. The best of color ... .20

D. M. MOORE—Very large, deep velvety maroon ... .50

GRAND DUKE ALEXIS—White edged lavender. Of distinct form and large size. Quilled petals ... .25

GETTYSBURG—Deep scarlet, large and free ... .10

GREAT BRITAIN—Beautiful lavender pink. A very large fluffy flower on good stems ... .75

HORTULANUS WITTE—Pure white. Very large. Another prize winner ... .50

HORTULANUS FIET—Salmon, yellow center. One of the largest. A prize winner. New ... .50

INSULINDE—Beautiful golden orange, very large flower on long stems ... 1.00

JACK ROSE—Identical in color with the rose of this name. Very free ... .10

JEANNE CHARMET—Lilac pink, shaded lighter toward the center. Long stems. Large and free. One of the best ... .15

J. M. GOODRICH—Medium size, long stems and very free. A beautiful salmon pink tipped yellow ... .30

KING OF AUTUMN—Well formed flower. Color, buff-yellow and terra cotta; unique in color, while stem and foliage show great vigor ... .75

LE GRAND MANITOU—One of the largest and most attractive Dahlias in existence. Pure white, striped deep reddish violet. The plant occasionally bears a solid violet flower. Free bloomer ... .20

MAD. A. LUMIERE—Pure white, tipped violet red. Very attractive. Free ... .25

MINA BURGLE—Rich brilliant scarlet. Very large on long stems. One of the best ... .25

MME. VAN DEN DAEL—White overlaid pink; very large flowers on long stems ... .25

MME. VICTOR VASSIER—Clear sulphur yellow. The best of its color ... .25

MAID OF KENT—Cherry red, tipped white ... .15

MME. HELEN CHARVET—Pure white. Very large ... .20

MOROCCO—Large, velvety maroon, tipped white ... .35

MRS. FLEERS—Salmon and rose. Good exhibition variety .25

MRS. ROOSEVELT—Pink, shading to soft pink. Large and free ... .35

MRS. C. H. BRECK—Soft yellow, suffused carmine pointed petals ... .60

MRS. WINTERS—Pure snow white. Perfect form ... .20

OBAN—Mauve. Perfect form ... .10

PERLE DE LYON—Pure white. The petals are cleft, giving the flowers an attractive appearance. Excellent for cutting ... .20

PAPA CHARMET—Brilliant coral red, hsaded velvety maroon. Very free ... .25

PRINCESS JULIANA—Pure white. Very long stems, medium size. Very free. The best white for cutting ... .20

PRINCE OF ORANGE—Orange, overlaid chrome yellow ... .15

PRINCESS VICTORIA LOUISE—Deep cerise, very free .. .50

PROF. MANSFIELD—Color varies from white to yellow, striped orange and red. Very large ... .25

SANTA CRUZ—Deep lemon yellow, overlaid salmon pink. Perfect form. Very large and free. New ... .60

SOUVENIR DE GUSTAVE DOUZON—A pleasing shade of

orange red. One of the very largest. Free............ .15
SYLVIA—Soft mauve pink, shaded white at the center. Good cut flower .... .15
TENOR ALVEREZ—Bronze red, penciled; velvety brown; very large .... .25
WM. AGNEW—Crimson scarlet. Large and free......... .15
W. W. RAWSON—Pure white overlaid amethyst blue. Somewhat resembles Grand Duke Alexis in form. Very large on long stems. One of the very best............ .30
YELLOW COLOSSE—Very large, pure yellow. One of the best of its color .... .30

Show Dahlias

ACQUISITION—Beautiful deep lilac. Very large, quilled petals .... .15
A. D. LIVONI—Soft pink, very free. One of the very best for cutting .... .15
ARABELLA—Sulphur yellow, tipped pink; very large and free .... .10
CALEB POWERS—Soft blush pink, very large and free.... .30
CHAMELEON—Flesh colored center, shading to crushed strawberry, with yellow tints. Large and free........ .20
CUBAN GIANT—Dark crimson.. Very large and free...... .20
DELIGHTED—Very large, pure white. The center is often elongated in a way to suggest the Roosevelt smile.. .35
DOROTHY PEACOCK—Clear pink. Large size and good form .... .25
DREER'S WHITE—Pure white. Nearly identical in form with "Grand Duke" .... .25
ELSIE BURGESS—White ground, tipped and suffused lavender; a very large flower on good stems; new........ .50
EUGENIE MIZARD—Yellow, shaded scarlet. Very large and compact .... .35
GLADIATEUR—Clear violet, shaded blue. Fine for exhibition .... .25
GLORIE DE LYON—One of the best pure white.......... .25
GRAND DUTCHESS MARIE—A large soft buff reverse side pink .... .35
LE COLOSSE—Very large, brick red, very popular........ 1.00
MAUD ADAMS—White overlaid delicate pink. Very large perfect form. One of the best new ones........... .35
MME. HEINE FURTADO—Pure white. Very large, perfect form .... .35
METEOR—Bright red. Very large .... .15
NORMA—Bright orange. Perfect form .... .20
PEARL—Lavender pink, tinted lighter. Very large and of perfect form .... .25
PRINCESS VICTORIA—Pure canary yellow, perfect form, long stems, very free .... .25
QUAKER LADY—Buff tipped white, very free .... .20
RED HUSSAR—Dazzling cardinal red. Very free. Very good cut flower variety .... .15
ROSE—Deep rose. Very large and free. One of the best.. .20
STANDARD—Dark chocolate. Very large. The best of its color .... .25
STORM KING—Pure white. Early and free .... .20
VIVIAN—White, edged rose violet, new and very choice.. .50
WHITE SWAN—Pearly white; free .... .15
YELLOW DUKE—Canary yellow, quilled petals. Very large .20

Fancy Dahlias

FRANK SMITH—Rich maroon, tipped white .... .25
GOLD MEDAL—Canary yellow, striped and flaked red.... .25
LUCY FAUCETT—Pale yellow, striped magenta. Very large and free .... .15
MRS. SAUNDERS—Yellow, tipped white. Very large.... .20

Pompon Dahlias

	Each
ALEWINE—Delicate pink, tinted lavender	.15
AMBER QUEEN—Clear amber, shaded apricot	.15
ARIEL—Buff tinted orange	.15
CATHERINE—Clear yellow. Very free	.15
FASHION—Orange	.15
GUIDING STAR—Pure white. Very free	.10
LITTLE BEAUTY—Soft pink	.15
LITTLE MABEL—Amber. One of the best	.15
PURE LOVE—Lavender blue, perfect form	.15
RAPHAEL—Very dark maroon. Fine form	.15
SNOWCLAD—Pure white	.20
SUNBEAM—Bright scarlet. Very fine	.15
SUNNY DAYBREAK—Apricot edged, rosy red	.25

Peony Flowered Dahlias

ATTRACTION—Very large, clear lilac rose, long stems	1.00
AVALANCHE—Pure white, large and of good form	.50
BERTHA VON SUTTNER—Salmon, shaded pink and rose. Very large and free	.35
BLOOMHAVEN—Beautiful light lavender; good for exhibition or cutting	1.00
CECELIA—Pale yellow. Very large. One of the best	.35
CHATENAY—Color similar to Chatenay rose; very beautiful on long stems	.50
DR. PERRY—Rich, dark mahogany. Very large. One of the best	.50
DUKE HENRY—Brilliant deep crimson; large and free	.20
ELSA—Fluffy white flowers on long stems	.50
GEISHA—Probably the showiest and most attractive dahlia in cultivation. The color is a brilliant scarlet and gold with a ring of clear yellow at the center	.50
GEISHA SUPURBA—An immense golden yellow suffused scarlet. Claimed to be an improved Geisha	.50
GLORY OF BAARN—Clear rose; very large	.20
HAMPTON COURT—Bright, deep pink, golden yellow center. One of the best	.20
HORTULANNUS BUDDE—Rich, rosy scarlet. Very large on long stems	.40
JOHN GREEN—Base of petals a clear golden yellow which quickly changes to a fiery scarlet. Petals are pointed. Very striking	.35
QUEEN EMMA—Rose pink, suffused yellow	.25
QUEEN WILHELMINA—Pure white; very large. The best white	.25
VAN DYKE—Old rose. Large flowers of decorative form	.50

Single Dahlias

BLANCHE—Very large, pale yellow at the base, faintly tipped pink and overcast white. Very free	.20
GOLDEN CENTURY—Golden yellow, shaded amber. Large on long stems	.20
20TH CENTURY—White at both base and tips, shading to rose pink at the center. Large	.15
ROSE PINK CENTURY—Deep pink; very large	.15
SCARLET CENTURY—Bright scarlet; very large	.20
SENSATION—Vermilion red, tipped white; very striking. Two rows of petals	.20
WHITE CENTURY—Pure white; very large	.20
SACHEM—Orange scarlet, very large, new	.35

Collarette Dahlias

MAURICE RIVOIRE—Rich crimson, pure white collar of short well formed petals. Very free on long stems..... .25

SOUVENIR DE CHAHANNE—Lemon yellow with coral-red markings. Collar petals long, lemon yellow, tipped white .... .25

We will send six of the varieties listed at 10 cents for 50 cents; six of those listed at 15 cents for 75 cents, etc. Prices quoted are for strong divisions of field grown roots, not rooted cuttings which are never as satisfactory. Dahlia roots at the each and dozen prices are sent postpaid.

Hardy Roses

CULTURAL DIRECTIONS—Roses prefer what is termed a deep clay loam soil. It should be well drained and away from the shade of trees and buildings. The soil should be deeply and thoroughly prepared and liberal applications of well rotted manure applied. The plants may be set eighteen inches apart in rows two feet apart. When planting budded bushes, the union of the bud and stock should come at least two inches below the surface of the soil. They should be planted as early in the spring as the soil is dry enough to work. After planting the shoots should be reduced to two or three and these cut back to at least four inches from the ground.

The stock we send out is 2-year-old, field grown. It is American grown and thoroughly acclimated to our soil and climate. Our stock of roses is first-class in every particular and should give a full crop of blooms two months after planting.

Hybrid Perpetual Roses

These are strong growing and generally hardy without protection. They produce a very abundant crop of large flowers in June and more or less continuously all summer.

Strong, 2-year-old, field grown plants, except where noted, 60 cents each, $6.50 per doz., six at dozen rates. Roses are sent by express, charges collect.

BARONESS ROTHSCHILD—A lovely light-pink; very large and of beautiful form.

CLIO—Flesh, shading to pink in the center. Very vigorous and free.

FRAU KARL DRUSCHKI—Produces perfectly formed blooms of pure white. The very best white rose for the garden.

GEN. JACQUEMINOT—Bright crimson scarlet, very fragrant. Very popular.

HUGH DICKSON—Crimson shaded scarlet, very large and full, long pointed buds. Very fragrant. One of the best.

J. B. CLARK—Deep scarlet, shaded darker. Very large.

M. P. WILDER—Bright carmine; very large, full and globular; free blooming and fragrant.

MRS. J. LAING—Soft pink, large full and of perfect form. The best pink garden rose.

PAUL NEYRON—Deep rose. Very large.

PRINCE CAMILLE DE ROHAN—Very deep velvety crimson. The best very dark rose.

ULRICH BRUNNER—Very large, rich crimson, good form and a reliable bloomer.

Everblooming Roses

These are the most important garden roses. They are the result of crossing tea roses with the hybrid perpetual roses. They combine the hardiness of the hybrid perpetual roses with the everblooming qualities of the tea roses. These will be benefited by some winter protection in the North.

ANNIE MULLER (Dwarf Polyantte)—Color bright pink, large clusters, continuous bloomer .... .60

BABY RAMBLER (Dwarf Polyantha)—Bright crimson. Blooms in clusters almost continuously. Dwarf bushy habit .... .60

DUCHESS OF WELLINGTON—Saffron yellow, flushed crimson, long pointed buds .... .80

ETOILE DE FRANCE—Velvety crimson, well formed bud, fragrant and free. 70c each.

GRUSS AN TEPLITZ—Bright crimson scarlet. Blooms in clusters and is very fragrant. One of the best bedding roses. 60c each.

GEO. DICKSON—An excellent new variety. A very vigorous grower and free bloomer. Dark crimson scarlet. Large and of fine form. The best red in its class. 75c each.

HARRY KIRK (Tea)—A true sulphur yellow. Very large long pointed buds. Fragrant and free. The best yellow rose. $1.00.

JONKHEER J. L. MOCK—New. Bright carmine changing to pink. Large, full and very fragrant. 80c each.

KAISERIN AUGUSTA VICTORIA—Pale primrose or creamy white. Large and full, elegantly formed buds. Very handsome. 80c each.

KILLARNEY—Flesh shaded pale pink, very handsome long pointed buds. Very fragrant. 70c. each.

LADY HILLINGTON (Tea)—Deep orange yellow, long pointed bud. Very free. 80c each.

LA FRANCE—Silvery rose pink. Large, full, handsomely formed and very fragrant. 70c each.

LYON ROSE—Coral-red shaded crome yellow. Very large and of good form. Free. 80c each.

MME. CAROLINE TESTOUT—Satiny rose, large and free, sweetly scented. 70c each.

MME. EDWARD HERRIOT (The Daily Mail Rose)—Deep reddish copper. Large and free. New and very choice. 90c each.

MADAM JULES GROLEZ—Beautiful china rose, large, full and of excellent form. One of the best. 80c each.

MAMAM COCHET (Tea)—Deep rose pink, inner side of petals silvery rose. Very strong growth and very free. Very large. 70c.

MRS. AARON WARD—Indian yellow shaded lighter towards the edges of the petals. Full, of good form and very free. 80c ea.

MY MARYLAND—Bright salmon pink. Very large, handsomely formed bud. Very fragrant and free. 75c each.

RADIANCE—Brilliant rose pink. Large, of fine form and very free. 70c each.

SUNBURST—Bronzy yellow, shaded apricot. Perfect form. Very choice. 90c each.

SOLEIL D'OR (Pernetiana)—Deep yellow shaded orange and red. Fine large globular flowers freely produced. Should not be pruned severely. 75c each.

WHITE KILLARNEY—Pure white. Form and growth like the parent. 70c each.

WHITE MAMAM COCHET (Tea)—Identical with its parent, Mamam Cochet, except in color. 70c each.

WM. R. SMITH—Creamy white, shaded, pink, long pointed bud and a reliable bloomer. 80c each.

Climbing Roses

CLIMBING AMERICAN BEAUTY—Deep rosy carmine, shaded rich crimson toward the center. Large, fragrant flowers. The plant is hardy and a vigorous grower. In great demand. 50c each.

CRIMSON RAMBLER—Crimson. Blooms in large clusters. Very popular. 50c each.

DOROTHY PERKINS—Soft pink. Blooms in large clusters. Very free. 50c each.

Peonies

CULTURE—Peonies should be planted from the beginning of September until the ground freezes. We begin digging early in September and can ship any time until the ground freezes. They prefer a heavy loam soil although any good garden soil will give good results. It should be well drained and away from the shade of trees or buildings. The soil should be worked deep. Manure should either be incorporated in the soil some time before the roots are planted or used as a mulch during winter and worked into the soil in the spring. It should not be allowed to come in contact with the roots at any time. The roots should be planted with the eyes two or three inches below the surface of the soil. They are hardy and free from insect attacks. Early planting is to be recommended at it gives the plants a chance to get established before the ground freezes. Orders may be booked at any time for fall delivery. As the stock of some of the new and rare varieties is limited, early orders are advisable.

So far as possible we send strong one-year old plants; when this is impossible, we send divisions with three to five strong eyes which generally bloom the first year. Peonies do not come to their best until the third or fourth year and some varieties do not bloom until the second or third year after planting. We grow our own roots and guarantee them true to name.

Abbreviations used for the introducer's name are: (And.), Anderson; (Cal.), Calot; (Cr.), Crouse; (Del.), Delache; (Des.), Dessert; (Gr.), Guerin; (**Kel.**), Kelway; (**Lem.**), Lemoine; (Miel), Miellez; (Rich.), Richardson; (Ros.), Rosefield; (Verd.), Verdier.

ACHILLE (Cal. 1844)—Large, rose type; shell pink fading to lilac-white. Fragrant, tall, free bloomer. 50c each.

ALBATRE (Cr. 1885)—Very large, compact rose type, milk white center, petals edged crimson. Fragrant, vigorous and very free. $1.50.

ALBERT CROUSE (Cr. 1864)—Very large bomb, rose-white flecked crimson. Fragrant and free, late. $1.00.

ALEXANDRE DUMAS (Gr. 1862)—Medium size, light violet rose, collar creamy white. Fragrant and free. 50c.

ALSACE-LORAINE (**Lem.** 1906)—Very large, semi-rose type creamy white shading to pale yellow. Vigorous and free. Late. $5.00.

ASA GRAY (Cr. 1886)—Very large, full semi-rose type. Delicate lilac, sprinkled with minute dots of deeper lilac, fragrant, very free. $1.00.

ATROSANGUINEA (Cal. 1850)—Medium size, semi-double. Brilliant rosy magenta, outer guards streaked white. Vigorous grower and a free bloomer. 50c.

AUGUSTIN D'HOUR (Cal. 1867)—Syn. Marechal MacMahon. Large bomb. Dark brilliant solferino-red, slight silvery reflex. Medium tall, free bloomer. 75c.

AVALANCHE (Cr. 1886)—Large, compact crwn. Milk-white, centre prominently flecked crimson. Fragrant and free. Late. Very choice. $1.00.

BARONESS SCHROEDER (Kel.)—Very large globular rose type. Flesh white. Very fragrant and free. One of the very best. $2.00.

BERNARD DE PALISSY (Cr. 1879)—Large, globular, rose type. Pale lilac rose, changing to nearly white with a blush center. Fragrant and free. Late. 50c.

CLAIRE DUBOIS (Cr. 1886)—Very large, globular, rose type. Clear deep violet rose. Late. $1.50.

COURONNE D'OR (Cal. 1872)—Large, semi-rose type. Pure white with a ring of yellow stamens around a tuft of center petals tipped carmine. Free. One of the best. 75c.

DELACHEI (Del. 1856)—Large rose type. Violet-crimson, strong grower and free bloomer. 50c.

DORCHESTER (Rich. 1870)—Large rose type. Pale hydrangea pink. Fragrant and free. Very late. Extra good. 50c.

DR. BRETONEAU (Verd. 1854)—Syn. Lady Leonora Bramwell. Large bomb. Pale lilac rose, Fragrant and free. Extra good for cutting. 35c.

DUCHESS DE NEMOURS (Cal. 1856)—Medium size. Pure white crown, sulphur white collar, no flecks. Fragrant and very free. Early. Extra good. 50c.

DUKE OF CLARENCE (Kelway)—Very large, globular crown. Guards violet-rose, collar cream-white, center flecked crimson. Frangrant. Tall. 75c.

EDULIS SUPERBA (Lemon 1824)—Large. Bright mauve pink. Very fragrant and free. Very early. One of the very best. 35c.

ELLA CHRITINE KELWAY (Kel.)—Very large full, rose type, soft lavander, very fragrant. $2.50 each.

ENCHANTRESS (Lem. 1903)—Very large, compact, rose type. Creamy white, fragrant. Strong grower. Very late. $10.00.

EUGENIE VERDIER (Cal. 1864)—Large, semi-rose type. Pale hydrangea pink, collar lighter, center deeply flecked crimson. Very free. Very late. 75c.

ETTA (Terry)—Very large, rose type. Pale hydrangea pink. Fragrant. Very late. $1.00.

FELIX CROUSSE (Cr. 1881)—Large, globular bomb. Brilliant red. Fragrant and free. One of the best reds. 75c.

FESTIVA (Donkalear 1838)—Very large, full rose type, pure white prominently flecked crimson, resembles Festiva Maxima, but is a more dwarf grower and later bloomer. 50c.

FESTIVA MAXIMA (Miel. 1851)—Very large, rose type. Pure white, center flecked crimson. Tall grower. Early. Extra good. 50c.

FLORAL TREASRE (Ros. 1900)—Very large, rose type. Pale lilac-rose. Fragrant and free. One of the best. 50c.

FRAGRANS (Banks 1805)—Often sold for Andre Lauries. Medium size bomb. Dark pink. Fragrant. Late. Extensively grown for cutting. 25c.

GOLDEN HARVEST (Ros. 1900)—Medium size bomb. Guards pale lilac-rose, center creamy white intermingled with pink. Fragrant and very free. 50c.

GRANDIFLORA (Rich. 1883)—Very large, rose type. Rose-white. Fragrant, tall, strong growers. One of the very best. $1.50.

GRANDIFLORA NIVEA PLENA (Lemon 1824)—Large globular rose type. Milk white. Very fragrant and very early. One of the best. 75c.

GROVER CLEVELAND (Terry)—Very large, rose type. Dark crimson. One of the best reds. Late. $2.00.

HUMEI (And. 1810)—Large, globular rose type. Cherry pink tipped silver. Fragrant. Very late. 25c.

KARL ROSENFELD (Ros. 1908)—Very large, compact, semi-rose type; dark crimson. Strong grower. One of the best reds. $4.00.

LADY ALEXANDER DUFF (Kel. 1902)—Very delicate, pale pink, central petals touched carmine. Large double flowers, very freely produced in clusters. $15.00.

LE GYGNE (Lem. 1907)—Very large, semi-rose type, petals incurved. Pure milk white, free bloomer, distinct and very beautiful. $20.00.

LA FRANCE (Lem. 1901)—Very large, compact, rose-type. Uniform, light rose color. Strong grower. Fragrant and free bloomer. One of the finest. $5.00.

LAMARTINE (Cal. 1860)—Syn. Gigantea. Very large, rose type. Pale lilac-rose. Fragrant and free. Choice variety. $1.00.

LIVINGSTONE (Cr. 1879)—Very large rose type. Pale lilac-rose, tipped silver, central petals flecked carmine. Free. Extra. $1.00.

LA TULIPE (Cal. 1872)—Very large, semi-rose type. Lilac-white, outer petals striped crimson. Fragrant and free. 75c.

LOUIS VAN HOUTTE (Cal. 1867)—Medium size, semi-rose type. Deep carmine rose, tipped silver. Very brilliant. Late. 35c.

MARIE LEMOINE (Cal. 1869)—Large, rose type. Pure white, center, cream-white tipped carmine. Fragrant. Very late. Extra. 75c.

MAD. BUCQUET (Des. 1888)—Large, semi-rose type. Very dark crimson amaranth. Fragrant and free. Very attractive. 75c.

MAD. CALOT (Miel. 1856)—Very large rose type. Pale hydrangea pink, center shaded darker, collar tinted silver. Fragrant and free. Early. 50c.

MAD. CROUSSE (Cal. 1866)—Medium size crown. Pure white, center flecked crimson. Free. Extra good. 50c.

MAD. DE VERNVILLE (Cr. 1885)—Large bomb. Pure white, center, blush when first open, flecked carmine. Fragrant and free. Early. Extra. 50c.

MAD. DUCEL (Mech. 1880)—Large, globular bomb. Light mauve rose, with silvery reflex. Fragrant and free. Extra. 75c.

MME. EMILE LEMOINE (Lemon 1899)—Semi-rose type, large and compact. Milk white. Very good. $1.50.

MAD. GEISSLER (Cr. 1880)—Very large, rose type. Violet-rose tipped silver. Very fragrant. Extra. 75c.

MILTON HILL (Rich.)—Very large, globular rose type. Pale lilac-rose. Late. One of the very finest. $3.00.

MODESTE GERIN (Gr. 1845)—Large, bomb. Uniform light solferino-red. Very fragrant and free. Extra. 50c.

MONSIEUR DUPONT (Cal. 1872)—Large, semi-rose type. Milk white, center splashed crimson. Fragrant and free. $1.00.

MONS. JLES ELIE (Cr. 1888)—Very large crown. Pale lilac-rose, collar lighter shaded amber yellow at the base. Fragrant. Early. Extra. $1.00.

MONS. KRELAGE (Cr. 1822)—Large, compact, semi-rose type. Dark solferino-red with silvery tips. Very free. Late. 75c.

MONS. MARTIN CAHUZAC (Des. 1899)—Medium size, semi-rose type. Very dark purple garnet with black reflex. The darkest peony in commerce. Very handsome. Free. $5.00.

OFFICINALIS RUBRA PLENA—Large, brilliant crimson. Very early. 35c.

PIERRE DESSERT (D. & M. 1890)—Very large, semi-rose type. Dark crimson purple. The largest and one of the earliest dark reds. $1.00.

PRINCESS BEATRICE (Kelway 1886)—Large, compact crown. Light violet-rose, collar cream-white, center flecked crimson. Very free. Extra. 50c.

RUBRA SUPERBA (Rich. 1871)—Large, compact rose type. Crimson. Very late. The very best late red. 75c.

SOULANGE (Lem. 1907)—Crown type, unusually large and full; outer petals lilac white, deepening toward center with salmon shading. Strong grower. Late. A very beautiful and distinct variety. $10.00.

SARAH BERNHARDT (Lem. 1906)—Semi-rose type; uniform rose-tipped silver; fragrant; very strong grower and very free. Late. $4.00.

SOUVENIR DE L'EXPOSITION UNIVERSELLE (Cal. 1867)—Very large, rose type, violet rose tipped silver, fragrant and free. $1.00.

THERISE (Des. 1904)—Very large rose type. Violet-rose shading lilac white in center. Strong grower, free bloomer. Very desirable. $6.00.

TOURANGELLE (Des. 1910)—Very large, rose type; salmon shaded rose white. Strong grower. Very attractive. $7.00.

TRIOMPHE DE L'EXPOSITION DE LILLIE (Cal. 1865)—Very large, compact, semi-rose type. Pale hydrangea pink, minutely splashed violet rose, guard petals fading to nearly white. Fragrant and free. Extra. 75c.

VENUS (Kelway)—Very large, compact crown. Pale hydrangea pink, collar lighter. Very fragrant and free. Extra. $1.50.

VIRGO MARIE (Cal. 1859)—Very large, bomb type, pure white. The genuine is very scare. $1.25.

WHITLEYI (Whit. 1808)—Medium size, globular bomb. Milk-white, guards slightly flecked crimson and tinted pale lilac. Fragrant and very free. Popular cut flower variety. 35c.

Single Peonies

ALBIFLORA (Des. 1902)—Very large; white with a tuft of long yellow stamens in center. Fragrant and very early. $2.00.

CLIO (Peterson 1901)—Vey large, light pink. The best single pink. $2.00.

MIKADO (Japan's Exhibit Chicago 1893)—Velvety-crimson guards enclose a filigree cushion of crimson petaloids edged and tipped gold, very attractive. $2.00.

DEFIANCE (Terry)—Bright, rich red. Very large and free. 75c.

German Iris

These are among the most delicately beautiful of the hardy perennials. They thrive in almost any soil or situation except that they cannot endure standing water. They may be planted in early spring, but best results are obtained by planting in August and September.

In the following descriptions, S. is for standards, or upper petals, and F. for falls or lower petals.

AGNES—S. White, frilled and shaded lilac; F. White, traced lilac. 2 ft., 10c.

FLAVESCENS—S. and F. Delicate soft yellow. Large, sweet scented. Early. 30 in., 10c.

FLORENTINA ALBA—Creamy white, fragrant. Early. 2 ft., 10c.

HER MAJESTY—S. Lovely rose pink; F. Bright crimson shaded darker. Very handsome. 20c.

HONORABILIS (Syn. Sans. Souci)—S. Golden yellow; F. Rich mahogany. 18 in., 10c.

INNOCENZA—Ivory white. 20 in., 20c.

IRIS KING—S. Clear lemon yellow; F. Rich maroon bordered yellow. Maori King X Pallida. Large and beautiful. 25c.

JACQUESIANA—S. Bright coppery crimson; F. Rich maroon. 30 in. Extra. 25c.

KHEDIVE—Soft lavender. 33 in., 15c.

LORELEY—S. Light yellow; F. Ultramarine blue bordered cream. 25c.

MAD. CHEREAU—White, elegantly frilled, clear blue. Very handsome. 32 in., 10c.

MAD. PAQUETTE—Bright rosy claret. 42 in. The best "red." 25c.

MAORI KING—S. Golden yellow; F. Velvety crimson margined gold. 18 in., 15c.

MRS. NEUBRONNER—Very deep golden yellow. The best clear yellow. 15c.

MRS. H. DARWIN—Pure white, falls slightly reticulated violet at base. One of the best whites. 2 ft., 15c.

NIEBELUNGEN—S. Fawn yellow; F. Violet purple suffused creamy white. New. 25c.
PALLIDA DALMATICA—S. Lavender; F. Deep lavender. A superb variety. 40 in., 25c.
PFAUENAGE—S. Olive gold; F. Plum color with gold border. Very beautiful. 10 in. New. 25c.
PLUMERI—S. Coppery rose; F. Velvety claret. 15c.
QUEEN OF MAY—Soft rose lilac, almost pink. 32 in., 15c.
RHEIN NIXE—S. Pure white; F. Deep violet blue edged white. Very attractive. New. 35c.
STENOPHYLA—S. Pale lilac; F. Violet. 10c.
VIOLACEA GRANDIFLORA—S. Rich blue; F. Violet blue. Large and handsome. 25c.

Intermediate Iris

Handsome new hybrids blooming between the dwarf and later blooming German Iris. They are all large flowering.

HALFDAN—Creamy white. 20c.
HELGE—Lemon yellow, shaded pearl. 25c.
IVORINE—Large creamy white. 20c.

Hardy Herbaceous Plants

The following list embraces the most desirable varieties of hardy perennial plants. They are all of easy culture and include some of the handsomest flowers in cultivation.

Unless noted, 20c each, $2.00 per dozen, by express.

ACHILLEA, THE PEARL—Small double white flowers in July. 1 ft.
ANEMONE, QUEEN CHARLOTTE—Large, semi-double, silvery pink. Oct.
A. WHIRLWIND—Very large, double white.
AQUILEGIA (Columbine)—Long spurred hybrids. The best in cultivation. All colors mixed.
CAMPANULA MEDIUM (Canterbury Bells)—Large, cup-shaped flowers, blue, rose and white mixed.
CHRYSANTHEMUM, HARDY POMPON—White, yellow, pink, crimson, bronze.
CONVALLARIA (Lily of the Valley)—25c each, $2.00 per dozen.
DELPHINIUM, BELLADONNA HYBRIDS—Clear turquoise blue flowers. Strong field grown roots. 25c each, $2.00 per dozen.
DIANTHUS BARBATUS (Sweet William)—Single. All colors mixed.
DIANTHUS PLUMARIUS—Hardy garden pinks. The old-fashioned fragrant variety. June.
DICENTRA, SPECTABILIS (Bleeding Heart)—Long racemes of graceful, pink, heart-shaped flowers. 25c each, $2.50 per doz.
DIGITALIS (Fox Glove)—Stately plants bearing long spikes of tubular flowers in July and August. 2 to 3 feet.
FUNKIA (Plaintain Day Lily)—Handsome broad foliage and fragrant lily-like flowers in late summer. 1 ft.
FUNKIA VARIEGATA—Leaves beautifully variegated white and green. Fine for edging. Dwarf. 25c. each, $2.00 per doz.
GAILLARDIA GRANDIFLORA—A fine large flowering strain; brown center, surrounded with crimson rings and yellow border. Continuously in bloom.
GYPSOPHILA PANICULATA (Baby's Breath)—Mist-like sprays of minute white flowers. Fine for bouquets.
HELLEBORS NIGER (Christmas Rose)—A dwarf hardy plant, bearing beautiful snow white, waxy flowers during mild days in winter, from December until Spring. Large clumps 35c each.
HEMEROCALIS FLAVA (Lemon Day Lily)—Fragrant, golden yellow flowers in large clusters. 2 feet.

HIBISCUS—New Giant flowering Marshmallow, or Mallow Marvels. Flowers sometimes 9 in. in diameter. Very hardy. 5 to 8 feet. Separate colors, red, pink and white. 25c each.

HOLLYHOCKS—Too well known to require description. All colors mixed.

IBERIS SEMPERVERNES—Hardy candytuft, evergreen foliage, completely covered with white flowers in May. 10 in.

PAPAVER ORIENTALE (Oriental Poppies)—Mixed hybrids. Scarlet shades. Large and showy.

PHLOX, HARDY—Select named varieties, 25c each. Standard varieties, 15c each, $1.50 per dozen, prepaid. By express, $9.00 per 100.

SHASTA DAISY—Large, snow white flowers throughout the fall. Splendid for cutting.

SPIREA JAPONICA Queen Alexandra—Soft, delicate pink. Feathery plumes. 25c.

SPIREA JAPONICA Gladstone—Similar to the above but pure white. 25c.

STOKESIA CYANEA (Stokes' Aster)—Large flowers of centaurea shape, and rich lavender-blue color. 18 in.

TRITOMA, PFITZERI (Red Hot Poker)—Long spikes of orange scarlet flowers, continuously from August to November. Very ornamental. 3 feet. 25c.

YUCCA FILAMENTOSA (Adams Needle)—Very stately both in foliage and flower. Creamy white. 3 feet. 25c each.

Hardy Shrubs

The following is a selected list of the most useful only. Parties desiring larger collections should write us:

BERBERIS THUNBERGII (Japanese Barberry)—Dwarf habit, small foliage changing to a beautiful red in Autumn. Makes a very handsome hedge. 30c each, $2.75 per dozen, $25.00 per 100.

BUDDELIA (Butterfly Bush)—Long panicles of reddish violet; fragrant flowers in summer. 35c.

DEUTZIA, PRIDE OF ROCHESTER—Large, double white flowers, back of petals slightly tinted rose. Flowers large in long panicles. Middle of June. 35c each, $3.00 per dozen.

FORSYTHIA FORTNEII (Golden Bell)—Bright yellow flowers, very early in spring. Foliage deep green. 35c each, $3.00 per dozen.

HIBISCUS (Rose of Sharon)—Very desirable ornamental shrubs flowering in August and September. Pink and white. 35c each, $3.50 per dozen.

HYDRANGEA PANICULATA GRANDIFLORA—White flowers in great pyramidal panicles in August and September. One of the best flowering shrubs in cultivation. 50c each, $5.00 per dozen.

LIGUSTRUM OVALIFOLIUM (California Privet)—A hardy shrub, glossy foliage almost evergreen. One of the best hedge plants. $1.50 per dozen, $4.00 per 100.

LONICERA FRAGRANTISSIMA (Fragrant Bush Honeysuckle)—Rich, dark green foliage, almost evergreen. Fragrant flowers in early spring. 50c.

PHILADELPHUS CORONARIUS (Sweet Syringa or Mock Orange)—Pure white, highly scented flowers early in the spring. 35c each, $3.00 per dozen.

SPIREA ANTHONY WATERER—Very bright crimson flowers, from June to October. Dwarf habit. 40c.

SPIREA PRUNIFOLIA FLORE PLENO (Bridal Wreath)—Pure white double flowers in May. Very desirable. 35c each, $3.00 per dozen.

SPIREA VAN HOUTEI—White flowers literally cover the plant in May and June. One of the finest flowering shrubs in cultivation. Makes a beautiful hedge. 35c each, $3.50 per dozen, $20.00 per 100.

SYRINGA VULGARIS (Common Lilac)—Bluish purple flowers, sweetly scented. 35c each, $3.00 per dozen.

SYRINGA VULGARIS ALBA (White Lilac)—Creamy white flowers. 40c each, $4.00 per dozen.

VIBURNUM OPOLUS STERILIS (Snowball)—Globular clusters of snow white flowers in May. Very satisfactory. 35c each, $3.00 per dozen.

VIBURNUM PLICATUM (Japanese Snowball)—White flowers. Very handsome foliage. 50c.

WEIGELIA EVA RATHKE—Deep reddish purple. Rather dwarf. 40c.

WEIGELIA ROSEA—Beautiful rose colored flowers in June. 35c each, $3.00 per dozen.

Hardy Climbing and Trailing Plants

AMPELOPSIS VEITCHII (Boston Ivy)—Grows very rapidly and clings to wall or fence forming a dense sheet of green foliage which changes to red in fall. Very popular for ornamentation of brick or stone structures. 50c each, $5.00 per doz.

ARISTOLCHIA SIPHO (Dutchman's Pipe)—A very handsome vine of rapid growth, very large, light green foliage and curious pipe-shaped yellowish brown flowers. 65c each.

CLEMATIS JACKMANI—Large, rich purple flowers, freely produced. Large, 2 year old plants, 60c each.

CLEMATIS PANICULATA—Pure white. The flowers are very fragrant and produced in great abundance in August. A rapid grower. Large 2 year old plants, 50c each.

ASTER PLANTS—Late branching white, shell pink, lavender and purple. Ready in May. 25c per dozen, $1.50 per 100, prepaid.

If bulbs or plants are required in large quantity, send me your list for special prices.

$2.35

one each of the above ten varieties prepaid for $2.00.

PEONIES—

Avalanche—White	$1.00
Dorchester—Light pink	.50
Eugenie Verdier—Pink	.75
Felix Crousse—Red	.75
Festiva Maxima—Early white	.50
Mons. Jules-Elie—Deep pink	1.00
	$4.50

One strong plant, each of the above six varieties of Peonies prepaid for $4.00.

One each of the 23 varieties of German Iris listed will be sent for $3.00, prepaid.

9 781528 208406